The LORD is My SHEPHERD

STUDY GUIDE

JOSHUA D. ROWE

D1193721

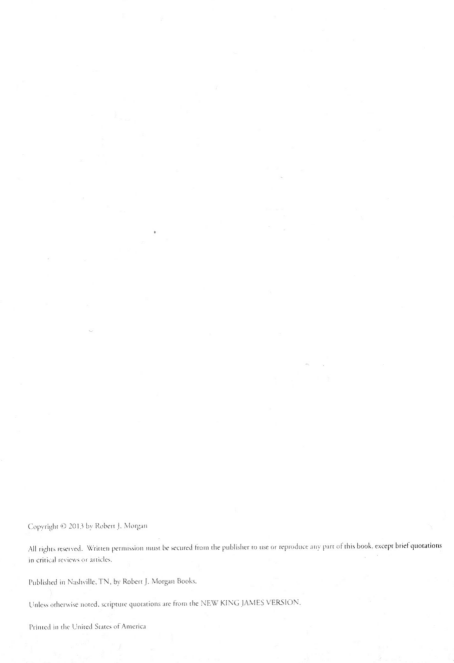

Published in Nashville, TN, by Robert J. Morgan Books.

Unless otherwise noted, scripture quotations are from the NEW KING JAMES VERSION.

Printed in the United States of America

CONTENTS

The
LORD
is My
SHEPHERD

Follow the Good Shepherd through Every Season of Life

Hello, my name is Joshua Rowe. Robert J. Morgan, the author of The Lord is My Shepherd, has mentored me since my teenage years, and now I'm privileged to join you as you study Psalm 23.

*Before we go any further, I feel compelled to ask a most important question: **Do you truly follow the Lord as your Shepherd?** If you're not sure, stop and read the final chapter of The Lord is My Shepherd entitled "Conclusion: The Shepherd is My Lord!" If you're studying Psalm 23 as a group, talk with your group leader about making a decision to follow Jesus Christ as Lord. If you're studying on your own, seek out a pastor or a Christian friend and talk with him or her about putting your faith in Jesus, the Good Shepherd. You can't fully benefit from a study of Psalm 23 until you've taken that step.*

I want to invite you to travel with me through meadows and trenches, through pathways and valleys, to high tablelands and a lavish palace. I want us to experience Psalm 23 as never before, and more, to engage the Lord as our Shepherd as never before.

Centuries ago, God's people, Israel, lived under the rule of a King named David whom God called a man after His own heart (1 Samuel 13:14; Acts 13:22). King David knew what it was like as a boy to shepherd sheep, and as a man to shepherd a nation. But it may surprise you that this capable shepherd and powerful king also knew what it was like to be a sheep. That's right, King David described himself as a sheep, knowing he was absolutely helpless without a shepherd to lead him. It was King David who penned the words, "The Lord is my shepherd" in the 23rd Psalm.

But these words weren't just for David! His poem was recorded in the book of Psalms, passed down through millennia, and alluded to by Jesus Christ Himself in John 10:10-11 when He said: "I am the good shepherd. The good shepherd gives his life for the sheep" (NKJV). And now this incredible Psalm has been given to us. The Lord isn't just King David's shepherd; He's my shepherd and your shepherd.

As our study of Psalm 23 progresses, we'll learn that our shepherd guides us in all aspects of life and provides for all the needs of life. The problem is, as Isaiah put it, we're prone to get lost: "We all, like sheep, have gone astray, each of us has turned to his own way..." (Isaiah 53:6; NIV84). We may try, but we aren't capable of navigating nor do we have the resources we need to deal with life's twists and turns.

Years ago when I was a Cub Scout, I mistakenly believed I could take my pocketknife and explore any terrain under any condition. It only took one scout trip to understand how little I really knew. The scout leader told us how dangerous the elements truly are. He introduced us to plants that looked edible, but could kill us. He taught us what snakes were venomous, how to prevent hypothermia, and why going out alone was never a good idea. At the end of one of these educational hikes, I grabbed a candy bar that made me sick (it had nuts inside I was allergic to) and I had to go home without camping. If I couldn't even weather a candy bar, how much less was I prepared to journey into the wilderness alone!

In the same way, alone we're completely helpless as we're exposed to this world. We may think we're ready for anything, but in fact we don't know the way nor do we have access to resources we need.

What about you? Do you feel overwhelmed with life's burdens? Are you typically unaware of God's blessings? Do you know what resources God offers you in your situation?

The alternative to a life lacking direction and resources is the life of a good sheep following a Good Shepherd—our lives as we follow Christ through every season of life. So if we're to be good sheep, our study through these 12 lessons should focus on following the Good Shepherd.

For each section we'll walk through a four-part lesson:

- *Survey the Shepherd's Land*
- *Hear the Shepherd's Voice*
- *Follow the Shepherd's Lead*
- *Remember the Shepherd's Goodness*

As I mentioned before, as a Cub Scout, it was important to be guided through different terrains and scenarios. You may not currently find yourself in the landscape described in a particular lesson so engage such lessons as preparation for the future.

SURVEY THE SHEPHERD'S LAND

To understand the structure of each lesson, think of yourself as a sheep. It may sound silly, but remember, this was the inspiration for the Psalm itself. We begin each lesson by surveying the Shepherd's land. Where do we find ourselves? In plentiful pastures? In difficult valleys? It's essential to first understand what landscape the Psalm is painting so we're able to recognize it in our lives. In these sections, we'll look deeply at our key verse and attempt to grasp its meaning.

HEAR THE SHEPHERD'S VOICE

Wherever we are, as sheep, we need guidance. We can't find our way alone. So we will hear the Shepherd's voice, focusing on Biblical texts and understanding more deeply what the Lord offers us as our shepherd through each step. In these sections, we'll dig deeper into the Psalm's meaning through cross references or deeper study, often with a particular focus or emphasis on Jesus.

FOLLOW THE SHEPHERD'S LEAD

Having heard His voice, we must now take action! It's fairly useless to hear the voice of a shepherd and stay put. So we're to follow the Shepherd's lead. We need to take a step of faith and apply the principles we've learned. In each lesson you'll have the opportunity to prayerfully commit to follow the Shepherd.

REMEMBER THE SHEPHERD'S GOODNESS

Unfortunately, our greatest journeys are quickly forgotten. With each step, we need to remember the Shepherd's goodness—to mentally process and physically record events, thoughts, and emotions. At the end of this guide, blank space is provided where you can journal your own reflections as you apply Psalm 23 to your life.

Along the way, please keep in mind some helpful notes and hints:

Don't worry that the length of each lesson may vary, and the length of each section within the lessons may also vary. It's not my intention to fill up space or to create perfect equilibrium. Instead, this study guide follows the book's lead in terms of content.

I've elected to use chapter numbers and headings as references when the book is referenced rather than page numbers. Sometimes a book's inner pages and associated page numbers are altered with reprints, and some electronic editions vary.

Make sure to carefully read all of the Scripture references in each lesson. Our transformation from wandering to following occurs when we apply biblical, rather than self-help principles.

Also, try to honestly answer each question. Some questions and answers may be uncomfortable or even painful. True transformation comes, however, only when we're honest with our Lord and ourselves.

In addition, please don't rush the process. You may spend extended time on one section. Just because we fill in the blanks doesn't mean we've taken the appropriate action. Allow the Lord and yourself time to process each step within you.

Finally, remember following the Good Shepherd through different seasons in life is not a one-time trip. We'll repeat and relive these steps throughout life. Hopefully, as we mature in Christ, we'll become increasingly obedient sheep, but it will be continual effort nonetheless.
Ready to join me in following the Good Shepherd?

Let's start here, by reading Psalm 23:

> *The Lord is my shepherd; I shall not want.*
> *He makes me to lie down in green pastures; He leads me beside the still waters.*
>
> *He restores my soul;*
> *He leads me in the paths of righteousness for His name's sake.*
> *Yea, though I walk through the valley of the shadow of death, I will fear no evil;*
> *For You are with me; Your rod and Your staff, they comfort me.*
> *You prepare a table before me in the presence of my enemies;*
> *You anoint my head with oil; my cup runs over.*
> *Surely goodness and mercy shall follow me all the days of my life.*
> *And I will dwell in the house of the Lord forever.*

Notice the green pastures, the still waters, the presence of enemies, the shadow of death, the house of the Lord. Whether you're experiencing green pastures and still waters or trudging through the valley of the shadow of death—whether enjoying blessings or enduring difficulty, the Lord is your shepherd, which is precisely what you need.

Which terrain do you feel you're currently experiencing?

How are you currently dealing with it? Are you noticing and praising God for blessings that surround you? Are you fearful or panicked in dark valleys or at the presence of enemies?

_____

_____

_____

Will you recognize Jesus as the Good Shepherd, and commit to follow Him (John 10:10–11)?

If you're ready, by faith, to follow the Good Shepherd, read through Psalm 23 at least twice and pray, committing yourself to Christ through this study. Pray in your own words, something like this:

> *Heavenly Father,*
> *You know how often I try to live in my own way, on my own strength. But I'm incapable of navigating through this life. I need you.*
>
> *Thank you, Jesus, for being the Good Shepherd. You laid down your life for me, but you also rose again so that, by the power of your Holy Spirit, you might shepherd your people. Please live through me as I commit myself to follow you all of my days. Thank you also for being not only the good shepherd but my shepherd.*
>
> *You know better than I the road I'm on, the blessings I miss, and the challenges I face. You also clearly see my condition. Don't let me be a stubborn sheep who won't listen, or a rebellious sheep who goes astray. Savior, like a shepherd, lead me.*
>
> *In Jesus' name, Amen.*

LESSON 1
GOD'S TRIAD OF TRUTH

Entrust the Good Shepherd with Your Past, Present, and Future

My 7-year-old son has Asperger's Syndrome. He's a delightfully intelligent little guy, but he tends to become overly stressed when his routines are threatened. Recently he was very upset because he hadn't finished his work quickly enough and, as a result, he missed part of recess at school. I told him not to let it bother him, but to move on and do better next time—but he couldn't let it go. When I suggested he had time to play outside presently, he didn't want to stop his current activity of drawing and "lose time". Finally I suggested he would have another chance tomorrow at school, but he worried that he might make the same mistake and miss recess again. It didn't matter what tense I attempted to help him address, he was in anguish over the past, the present, and the future!

I realized this isn't something unique to a child with Asperger's. We all tend to lament past mistakes. We fret about the situation we're in now. We worry about what the future holds.

Which affects you the most: are you haunted by your past, struggling with your present situation, or worried about the future?

_____

_____

Why?

_____

_____

Whatever stress you're experiencing, our lesson introduces us to God's answer to our past, our present, and our future, in what Rob Morgan calls:

God's Triad of Truth.

Let's explore this truth in more detail.

SURVEY THE SHEPHERD'S LAND

Read the chapter entitled *Introduction* in *The Lord is My Shepherd.*

Read Psalm 22—24.

Why does Morgan call this a "Messianic trilogy"?

_____

_____

What is the primary setting and subject of Psalm 22?

_____

_____

What is the primary setting and subject of Psalm 23?

_____

_____

What is the primary setting and subject of Psalm 24?

_____

_____

HEAR THE SHEPHERD'S VOICE

This trilogy of Psalms describes Jesus as our Suffering Savior, as our Loving Shepherd, and as our Reigning King. Morgan suggests this is the answer to our past, present, and future.

Based on Psalm 22, Morgan says "the savior's cross takes care of yesterday". How does this correspond with Colossians 2:13–14 and 1 Peter 2:24–25?

_____

_____

_____

Morgan explains that Psalm 23 teaches us "the shepherd's crook takes care of today".

Read John 10:1–16 and Hebrews 13:20–21.

How is Jesus' role as our Shepherd related to our daily needs?

_____

_____

_____

According to Psalm 24, Morgan explains, "the sovereign's crown takes care of tomorrow". Take a moment to read the following sections. Take at least 2–3 minutes to meditate on each:

Read 24:1–2 and meditate on the greatness of the Creator.

Read 24:3–6 and meditate on the privilege of coming into His presence in worship.

Read 24:7–10 and meditate on the nearing day when the King will come to claim His Kingdom.

How does your mind react when you're focused on these truths?

_____

_____

_____

_____

FOLLOW THE SHEPHERD'S LEAD

As we prepare to follow the Good Shepherd through different seasons of life, we need to acknowledge that, as Rob puts it, "Tension comes in three tenses".

Which of the following emotions do you typically experience when thinking about your past? What about your present? Your future? Circle all that apply:

anxiousness	nervousness	fear	regret
uncertainty	frustration	panic	depression
sadness	despondency	anger	

How does embracing God's Triad of Truth affect your response?

_____

_____

_____

_____

REMEMBER THE SHEPHERD'S GOODNESS

In light of this first lesson, record a journal entry that includes reactions and your intended response to what you've learned. Blank journal pages are provided for Lesson #1 beginning on page 75 in the back of this study guide.

> *Heavenly Father,*
> *My past is full of mistakes, but your Cross is a picture of forgiveness. My current situation is full of stress and difficulty, but I want to follow you as my Shepherd. Please guide and provide in this season of life. I often worry about the future—help me envision Jesus who will sit on the throne throughout eternity. I commit my past, my present, and my future to Jesus, the Good Shepherd.*
>
> *In Jesus' name, Amen*

"Our Shepherd holds us safely, and He alone can take care of our past, our present, and our future..."
—Robert J. Morgan

The LORD is My SHEPHERD

STUDY GUIDE

The
LORD
is My
SHEPHERD

LESSON 2

GET TO KNOW THE LORD AS YOUR SHEPHERD

The Lord is my Shepherd, I shall not want

Preparing a child for her first day of school is challenging and fascinating. One of the biggest hurdles is explaining the role of her teacher. Parents must explain this new role: "Now honey, you need to obey the teacher because she's in charge. But you can also ask her for help if you have trouble with anything." Introducing the role of this new figure in a child's life is crucial, so she's able to properly follow the teacher's lead and rely on the teacher for support.

In the same way, it's probably a new perspective for us as we begin to look at Jesus Christ, our savior, the king of the universe, as *our* shepherd. Even if we've been aware of Scriptures ascribing this role to Him—we're now embarking on a journey with Him, committing ourselves as His faithful flock. Before we're able to go very far, we need to acquaint ourselves more fully with the role of the Lord as our shepherd, and our role as His sheep.

What are the first things that come to mind when you try to envision the Lord as your shepherd?

What needs do you currently have that a good shepherd may be able to supply?

Whatever situation you're facing, one thing is certain: you need the Good Shepherd. And the good news is, you have one. As verse 1 of Psalm 23 reads:

The Lord is My Shepherd.

Let's get to know Him more together.

Survey the Shepherd's Land

Read chapters 1—3 in *The Lord is My Shepherd*.

Read Psalm 23:1 several times.

What is the significance of David's use of Yahweh, the proper and personal name of God?

_____

_____

_____

_____

In the original language of the New Testament, Jesus Christ is given the title "Lord".

How does this impact our understanding of Psalm 23?

_____

_____

_____

_____

What tense (past, present, or future) is verse 1 written in? Why is this significant?

_____

_____

_____

_____

What's the significance of the personal pronoun "my" in verse 1?

_____

_____

_____

_____

How does Pastor Morgan describe sheep? How does this impact our role to the Lord as our shepherd?

_____

_____

_____

Morgan writes, "Of course, the word want is used in its archaic sense here. It doesn't mean that if the Lord's our Shepherd we'll have everything we want. It means we'll not want for anything we need." With this in mind, rewrite verse 1 in your own words:

_____

_____

_____

_____

Hear the Shepherd's Voice

Pastor Morgan teaches that every word in this first verse is full of rich meaning and application. Let's dig deeper into verse 1 as we continue to learn about the Lord in His role as our shepherd.

King David, writing Psalm 23, begins "The Lord". He was meditating on *who* God is. Read Philippians 4:8.

What implications do these admonitions have on your relationship with God?

_____

_____

_____

_____

We noted earlier that Psalm 23:1 is written in the present tense: The Lord is my shepherd. Read the following Scriptures, noting the word "is" or "am" in the present tense:

> *Genesis 28:16*
> *Exodus 15:2*
> *Deuteronomy 33:27*
> *Psalm 27:1*
> *Psalm 46:1*
> *Habakkuk 2:19*
> *1 Corinthians 1:9*
> *1 Corinthians 1:25*
> *1 Corinthians 3:17*
> *Romans 8:31*
> *2 Corinthians 9:8*
> *John 8:58*
> *John 6:35, 8:12, 10:9, 10:11, 11:25*

What impact do these verses have on your understanding of God?

_____

_____

_____

Rob teaches us that the Lord isn't just *a* shepherd; he's *my* shepherd.

Take a moment to circle all the personal pronouns that refer to God (He, my, I, your, you, etc.) in Psalm 23:

> *The Lord is my shepherd; I shall not want.*

> *He makes me to lie down in green pastures; He leads me beside the still waters.*

> *He restores my soul;*

> *He leads me in the paths of righteousness for His name's sake.*

11

Yea, though I walk through the valley of the shadow of death, I will fear no evil;

For You are with me; Your rod and Your staff, they comfort me.

You prepare a table before me in the presence of my enemies;

You anoint my head with oil; my cup runs over.

Surely goodness and mercy shall follow me all the days of my life.

And I will dwell in the house of the Lord forever.

How does this inform and impact your relationship to the Lord as shepherd?

_____

_____

_____

_____

Read Isaiah 53:6 and Matthew 9:36.

How do we tend to be like sheep in a negative way? How does a shepherd change that paradigm?

_____

_____

_____

_____

Morgan explains that Psalm 23:1 could also be written, "Because the Lord is my shepherd, I shall not lack anything".

Read the following Scriptures and meditate on the Lord's promises of provision:

Matthew 6:32–33
Psalm 34:9
Philippians 4:19
2 Corinthians 9:8
Psalm 84:11
2 Corinthians 9:8

FOLLOW THE SHEPHERD'S LEAD

To summarize, we've learned the importance on meditating on who God is; we've understood the present reality of Jesus as our shepherd; we've seen how personal the shepherd is; and we've explored our role as sheep and the role of Jesus as leader and provider—as our shepherd.

Now let's put these ideas into practice.

Read 1 Timothy 1:17, then take at least 2–3 minutes to stop and meditate on this verse. Record your reactions:

_____

_____

_____

_____

How can you better integrate meditation on who God is into your daily routine?

_____

_____

_____

_____

Concerning the present tense of Psalm 23:1, Morgan writes, "It's not a promise to claim, but a reality to experience. Our Lord is a Shepherd whose presence is instant, immediate, and accessible every day, every hour, every moment".

Thinking of your present situation, how can you live out this truth today?

_____

_____

_____

_____

Read the following lines a few times out loud, placing emphasis on the word(s) in bold, pausing to reflect on the implications of each word.

The Lord *is my Shepherd*
The Lord **is** *my Shepherd*
The Lord is **my** *Shepherd*
The Lord is my **Shepherd**

We often focus on what we don't have.

Instead, take a moment to focus on the phrase "I shall not want". With your understanding of the Lord as shepherd, record some of the ways He's currently leading you and providing for your needs:

_____

_____

_____

_____

REMEMBER THE SHEPHERD'S GOODNESS

In light of this lesson, record a vivid journal entry describing the implications verse 1 has on your life this very day, right now. Blank journal pages are provided for Lesson #2 beginning on page 77 in the back of this study guide.

Heavenly Father,
Help me to understand what it truly means to be a good follower of Jesus. Help me fully see and understand Your role as my shepherd today. Would you provide for my needs and enable me to see and give praise to You when they've been met? Teach me today and throughout my life how all my needs are met in Christ, that I might not grasp for anything else.
In Jesus' name, Amen

"Everything is summed up in Psalm 23:1 and in its imagery of God's shepherding care: 'Because the Lord is my shepherd, I have everything I need.'"
—Robert J. Morgan

The LORD is My SHEPHERD

STUDY GUIDE

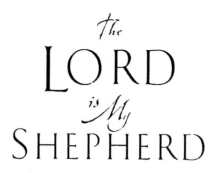

The
LORD
is My
SHEPHERD

LESSON 3

HIS PEACE IN LIFE'S MEADOWS

He makes me to lie down in green pastures;
He leads me beside the still waters

My brother-in-law measures in at 6'11" (and three-quarters). His last name is Webster, so his football buddies called him "Dub", abbreviating for the "W" in his last name. I wouldn't want to face off with him on the opposing line. What's intriguing to me is how aware of this fact his children are. They've never seen anyone bigger or more imposing than their father, and they seem to barrel through life unafraid of anyone. Because "Dub" is their dad, they know there are few who will bother them!

Similarly, Rob Morgan poses that, because the Lord is our shepherd, we have everything we need! He teaches that everything following verse 1 details how all our needs are met, regardless of our situation, because the Lord is our Shepherd.

Verse 2, then, is a pivotal verse for our study. Now we're following our Shepherd's lead into various territories! We'll learn how to more fully lean on His leadership and resources as we take this journey together.

Verse 2 begins with a serene word picture of the Lord's leading you, his sheep, into green pastures and beside still waters.

17

Even if you're dealing with difficulty, what areas of your life would you characterize as peaceful?

_____

_____

_____

_____

How are you reacting to the peace and provision in your life?

_____

_____

_____

_____

Whether your life is surrounded by peace and tranquility, or you're only experiencing small areas of peace Psalm 23:2 teaches us:

He makes me to lie down in green pastures; He leads me beside the still waters.

Let's walk together through this picture of the meadows of life.

SURVEY THE SHEPHERD'S LAND

Read chapter 4 in *The Lord is My Shepherd.*

Read Psalm 23:2 several times.

Rob asks the question: "…while these four words in verse 2—green pastures, still waters—conjure up a beautiful scene in our minds, what exactly is the meaning of it?" He suggests three levels of meaning.

To re-emphasize each point in your mind, scan through chapter 4 and fill in the blanks:

1. This is a Picture of _____:

    Our _____ are _____

2. This is a Picture of _____:

    Our _____ are _____

3. This is a Picture of _____ _____:

    Our _____ are _____

What's the significance of the words "lie down" in verse 2?

_____

_____

_____

_____

What's the significance of pastures and water to the life of a sheep?

_____

_____

_____

_____

Notice the two main adjectives in verse 2: "green" and "still". How do these words impact the picture in our minds?

_____

_____

_____

_____

Morgan writes: "Psalm 23 is an allegory. We're not talking about real sheep or a real shepherd; we're talking about a beautiful oil painting that hangs in the gallery of our minds to illustrate a real truth."

What "real truth" do you think verse 2 conveys?

_____

_____

_____

_____

Hear the Shepherd's Voice

Does the Lord truly and consistently meet our needs, give us peace, and nourish our soul? Let's explore these Scriptural ideas in more detail.

Read John 10:9–11.

What's Jesus referring to when he promises that His sheep will find pasture?

_____

_____

_____

Read Matthew 6:25–33. Think of the physical need you worry most about.

Does this Scripture cover that need with a promise to provide?

_____

Would you describe your life as peaceful? Why or why not?

_____

_____

_____

Take at least a few moments to read and meditate on the following verses:

- *Isaiah 30:15*
- *Job 34:29*
- *Isaiah 7:4*
- *Isaiah 32:17*
- *Philippians 3:11–13*
- *Proverbs 15:15*
- *Hebrews 13:5*
- *1 Thessalonians 4:11*
- *1 Peter 3:4*
- *1 Timothy 6:6*

Which verse strikes speaks to your current situation most poignantly?

_____

_____

Rob notes that we need more than just physical nourishment; our souls need to be fed also. Read Jeremiah 3:15, 23:10, and 23:16–22.

What kind of "pasture" does the Lord desire His sheep to enjoy?

_____

_____

Pastor Morgan writes, "Meditation is the practice of chewing on a verse we've previously read, memorized, or studied until we digest it. It's the process of masticating a Scripture until it's broken down and assimilated throughout our souls."

Read the following passages about meditation:

- *Genesis 24:63*
- *Joshua 1:8*
- *Psalm 1*
- *Psalm 49:3*
- *Psalm 119:15, 27, 48, 78, 97, 99*

Is meditation currently incorporated into your daily routine?

_____

Pastor Morgan makes a correlation between the "still water" and the Holy Spirit we need for illumination and guidance.

Read John 7:37–38, 14:26; 1 Corinthians 2:12, and Psalm 119:18 and record your thoughts:

_____

_____

_____

_____

FOLLOW THE SHEPHERD'S LEAD

The Lord leads us to green pastures and still waters, providing for our needs and granting us peace and nourishment. However, in the busy-ness of our lives, it's easy to overlook His provision. Let's take a moment to recognize the green pastures and still waters available to us.

What blessings in your life can you identify as God's provision?

_____

_____

_____

_____

Take a moment to say a prayer of thanksgiving for these blessings.

Morgan writes:

> *Instead of reminding yourself of what you crave, remind yourself of what you have. Build some quiet zones into your routine. Learn the sound of silence. Make time to rest your weary mind and body. Take time for prayer and contemplation. Reduce your wants. Increase your joys. And be thankful.*

How can you put this exhortation into practice in your life?

_____

_____

_____

_____

Write out a plan to incorporate meditation and a reliance on the Holy Spirit into your daily routine?

_____

_____

_____

_____

REMEMBER THE SHEPHERD'S GOODNESS

In light of this lesson, write a journal entry that records your interaction with this verse and its impact on your life. If you're artist, consider drawing out the scenery of verse 2 and write up an explanation of how it relates to you as a sheep following the Good Shepherd. Blank journal pages are provided for Lesson #3 beginning on page 79 in the back of this study guide.

> *Heavenly Father,*
> *Whether I'm always able to recognize it or not, You consistently lead me to green pastures and quiet waters. You've provided for my physical needs, my emotional needs, and my spiritual needs. Help me to continually feast on your Word and to drink deeply of the Holy Spirit.*
> *In Jesus' name, Amen*

"Green pastures and still waters have never been as available as they are to us right now. Because the Lord is our Shepherd, we have His peace in life's meadows." —Robert J. Morgan

The
LORD
is My
SHEPHERD

LESSON 4

HIS POWER IN LIFE'S TRENCHES

He restores my soul

A few years back, I tried to encourage a friend who had recently experienced a terrible turn of events. He had sunk into depression and bad habits. He told me, "I feel like I've just fallen off a ledge and there's just no hope for me to pull myself back up."

Rob Morgan asks us if we can relate to this type of thinking: "Are you cast down? Is your world upside down? Are you unable to right yourself? We so frequently need this tiny phrase of four words in Psalm 23:3: 'He restores my soul'".

What are you experiencing right now that has you feeling cast down?

_____

_____

_____

_____

How have you attempted to deal with this circumstance?

_____

_____

_____

_____

We're prone to, like my friend, attempt to "pull ourselves back up", but Psalm 23:3 has a different approach that relies on the Lord as our shepherd:

He restores my soul.

Let's look at how the Shepherd restores us.

SURVEY THE SHEPHERD'S LAND

Read chapter 5 in The Lord is My Shepherd.

Read the first phrase in Psalm 23:3 several times.

Considering the imagery of Psalm 23, what situation might a sheep find itself in that would require it to be restored?

_____

_____

_____

How might a shepherd restore a sheep that's been cast down?

_____

_____

_____

_____

Rob suggests three ways in which the Lord restores us. To re-emphasize each point in your mind, scan through chapter 5 and fill in the blanks:

   1. He Restores from *Sin*

   2. He Restores from *Stress*

   3. He Restores from *Sorrow*

HEAR THE SHEPHERD'S VOICE

How does the Lord restore His people? Let's explore this concept in more detail.

Read Psalm 119:176.

What roles are described here in terms of the sheep and the shepherd?

_____

_____

Describe the role of the Lord as shepherd in Ezekiel 34:11:

_____

_____

_____

Morgan suggests we, like sheep, are often cast down because of sin. Should past sins continue to haunt you as a believer?

Read the following passages and then respond with your thoughts:

> *Micah 7:19*
> *Isaiah 1:18*
> *Psalm 103:12*
> *Colossians 2:14*
> *Job 14:17*
> *Isaiah 38:17, 44:22*

_____

_____

_____

_____

Not only sin, but stress often casts us down.

Read Psalm 119:25, 37, 40, 88, and 107.

In what ways does the Psalmist ask the Lord to "revive" (NKJV) him?

_____

_____

_____

Sorrow often weighs us down as members of the Lord's flock. How does our shepherd restore us through seasons of sorrow?

Read John 14:1–3 and 2 Corinthians 1:3–4 and respond with your thoughts:

_____

_____

_____

FOLLOW THE SHEPHERD'S LEAD

All of us need seasons of restoration in our lives. Sometimes it means having the burden of guilt over our sin lifted. Other times it means enjoying a reprieve from life's stress. Still other times we need relief from the sorrows that accompany this sinful world.

In your situation, what do you feel you need to be restored from? Circle all that apply:

Sin   Stress   Sorrow

Explain:

_____

_____

_____

_____

If you feel burdened by the guilt of past sins, first take a moment (if you haven't already) to repent, to plea the blood of Jesus Christ to cover your transgressions, and to accept His forgiveness and grace. If there's anyone you need to make amends with, stop this study and do so if possible.

Now take a moment to choose a verse from the list below and commit it to memory (or write it on a note card to take with you):

Micah 7:19
Isaiah 1:18
Psalm 103:12
Colossians 2:14
Job 14:17
Isaiah 38:17, 44:22

If you're burdened by stress, read the story from chapter 5 again under the heading "He Restores from Stress". This story is very personal to me, because it's about my youngest son from my wife's perspective.

What stress can you lay down right now at the shepherd's feet and entrust to His care?

_____

_____

_____

_____

If you're burdened with great sorrow, write out a prayer to the Lord, laying your burden at His feet and asking for His comfort:

_____

_____

_____

_____

_____

_____

_____

_____

REMEMBER THE SHEPHERD'S GOODNESS

Write a journal entry that details the primary area you need the Lord to restore you. Blank journal pages are provided for Lesson #4 beginning on page 81 in the back of this study guide.

Interact with the phrase "He restores my soul" and record your thoughts and reactions.

_____

_____

_____

_____

_____

Heavenly Father,

My flesh wars against my spirit, and sin so easily entangles me. Lead me not into temptation, but deliver me from evil. Forgive me for my sin, and release me from guilt because of the price Jesus paid on the cross. As Jesus warned, in this world I do and I will have trouble. Please restore my soul, grant me peace in the midst of adversity. Sometimes sorrow comes unexpectedly, and sometimes it's a daily reality. Lord, you know what it's like to live in this world filled with the reality of death and grave sorrow. Comfort and restore me, and fill me with the joy of the Holy Spirit.

In Jesus' name, Amen

"For thus says the Lord God: 'Indeed I Myself will search for My sheep and seek them out'" (Ezekiel 34:11).

The LORD is My SHEPHERD

STUDY GUIDE

LORD
is My
SHEPHERD

LESSON 5

HIS PLAN FOR LIFE'S PATHWAYS

He leads me in paths of righteousness for
His name's sake

I had the pleasure of visiting Israel with Rob Morgan. On the evening we arrived, after a sleepless overseas flight for me, Rob suggested we go for a walk in the Old City. Too tired to navigate, I asked him to lead us back to the hotel; he got us incredibly lost. I wasn't too upset because we share a stunning directional deficiency. So, a few days later, I accidentally returned the favor. After a long day with Rob leading our group, we went off on our own to explore. On the walk back to our hotel, Rob said, "you lead the way, I'm just too tired." In our tourist clothes including shorts and short-sleeves, I inadvertently led us through a very traditional Jewish section of town. Posted on a wall was this plea: "For God's sake, please don't wear shorts!" I certainly didn't lead us down the right path, and according to that particular community, we weren't displaying acceptable righteousness in our attire as we travelled along their path!

Pastor Morgan writes that the phrase "paths of righteousness" has a dual meaning: "First paths of righteousness are *right* paths. They are right for you and me, and they represent those decisions and directions that will fulfill God's preordained will for me...Second they are *righteous* paths; they represent a daily walk that is pleasing to God". Do you long to be led down that kind of path?

Can you see the Lord's hand in leading you down your current path?

_____

_____

_____

Is your current path is both right and righteous, both providential and pleasing?

_____

_____

_____

Sometimes it's difficult for us to see God's direction in our lives and how it could work out for our good and His glory. But the truth we're told in the second part of Psalm 23:3 is:

He leads me in paths of righteousness for His name's sake.

Let's look at both our guide and our path together.

SURVEY THE SHEPHERD'S LAND

Read chapter 6 in *The Lord is My Shepherd.*

Read Psalm 23:3 several times.

Is the scene in Psalm 23 stationary or an excursion? What leads you to this conclusion?

_____

_____

_____

In what ways does a literal shepherd utilize qualities of a leader?

_____

_____

_____

Rob makes a few suggestions as to the leadership skills required of a biblical shepherd:

Foresight

Advance planning

Negotiating skills and diplomacy

Geographical skills

Business savvy

Stamina

Quality control

Hard work

Motivation

Emergency

Humility

Circle the qualities above that also describe God as our shepherd.

Now re-read the same qualities and additionally circle the qualities Jesus displayed in His life and ministry.

Rewrite the phrase "He leads me in paths of righteousness for his name's sake" in your own words:

_____

_____

HEAR THE SHEPHERD'S VOICE

Rob suggests that Psalm 23 retraces Genesis 37 to illuminate that Psalm 23 is a "circuit" or a journey.

What implications does this have on your understanding of Psalm 23?

_____

_____

_____

Read the following passages and describe the relationship between God's leading and our paths:

    Proverbs 3:5–6
    Psalm 32:8
    Psalm 37:23
    Psalm 48:14
    Psalm 73:24
    Psalm 139:16
    Isaiah 48:17
    Isaiah 58:11

_____

_____

_____

_____

_____

_____

FOLLOW THE SHEPHERD'S LEAD

This lesson is probably the most application heavy since Rob lays out an excellent plan of action to help us follow the Good Shepherd down life's pathways.

Rob exhorts us to "sail on the seven C's of Divine Guidance". So let's "sail the C's" together.

What paths lie ahead of you that leave you in need of guidance?

_____

_____

_____

_____

*1. Write out a prayer, **Committing** your decision to the Lord:*

_____

_____

_____

_____

_____

*2. Rob urges us to open the **Covers** of the Bible and seek Scriptural direction. Have you sanctioned off a portion of each day for reading the Scriptures? If not, write down a daily time you can commit to doing so:*

_____

3. What person (or people) in your life could offer you wise **Counsel**? Read Proverbs 15:22 and write the name(s) below, committing to contact them with your concerns.

_____

_____

4. Read Ruth 3:18 and Exodus 2:4, then answer the question: how are the **Circumstances** leading?

_____

_____

5. Take a moment to search yourself to see if an inner **Conviction** has begun to develop. Record your thoughts:

_____

_____

_____

6. Take some time to **Contemplate** the issue. Use your God-given logic to weigh pro's and cons:

_____

_____

_____

7. **Commit** *yourself to be content with the way God leads. Write a prayer, submitting yourself to obeying however He leads:*

_____

_____

_____

_____

REMEMBER THE SHEPHERD'S GOODNESS

Spend some time looking at the pathways that lie ahead of you.

Write a journal entry detailing how Psalm 23:3 impacts your understanding of the situation. Blank journal pages are provided for Lesson #5 beginning on page 83 in the back of this study guide.

Heavenly Father,
Thank you for leading me on a journey rather than allowing me to stagnate. Thank you that Jesus has walked on the earth and understands my struggles and weaknesses. I pray, as He did, let Your will be done. Lead me, and teach me to hear your voice and to respond obediently.
In Jesus' name, Amen

"My sheep hear my voice, and I know them, and they follow Me"
(John 10:27, NKJV).

The LORD is My SHEPHERD

STUDY GUIDE

THE LORD IS MY SHEPHERD

LESSON 6

HIS PRESENCE IN LIFE'S VALLEYS

Yea, though I walk through the valley of the shadow of death, I will fear no evil; For You are with me; Your rod and Your staff, they comfort me.

As a kid, I remember once visiting Mammoth Cave. Our guide walked us through, pointing out all the dangers encountered by the first explorers. The most memorable portion of the tour was when the guide said, "hit the lights" to her assistant, and everything went completely, utterly black. I couldn't see my hand inches in front of my face. Of course, the workers there conduct hundreds of such tours, and tourists all make it through the cave to the other side. But I couldn't help but wonder, what if I were to enter that cave alone with no guide and no light?

Thankfully, we have a shepherd who guides our steps and lights our paths through life's darkest valleys.

What "valley" or difficulty are you currently walking through?

_____

_____

Are you reacting with fear or are you experiencing the Lord's comfort?

_____

If you're currently going through a difficult time, and you find yourself in a deep valley, the good news is that the Lord will shepherd you through it. It's temporary, and you're not alone. Psalm 23:4 assures us:

Yea, though I walk through the valley of the shadow of death, I will fear no evil; For you are with me; Your rod and Your staff, they comfort me.

Let's learn about the presence and comfort of our shepherd through life's valleys.

SURVEY THE SHEPHERD'S LAND

Read chapter 7 in *The Lord is My Shepherd*.

Read Psalm 23:4 several times.

We've been labeling this section in each study "Survey the *Shepherd's* Land" with the understanding that the Lord is sovereign over the universe.

When we come to verse 4, does it seem inappropriate to you that we're calling this "The Shepherd's Land"? Why or why not?

_____

_____

_____

Pastor Morgan notes that many speculate that the Wadi Kelt was the specific gorge in David's mind as he penned this line of the poem. He explains this as the route Jesus would have taken in biblical times as He left Galilee. This gorge is the setting of the story of the Good Samaritan in Luke 10:30–37.

Read this passage and note the elements of danger pervading this valley:

_____

_____

_____

Notice the first word of Psalm 23:4: "Yea". Morgan points out this means "yes" and connects verse 3 to verse 4.

What's the significance of linking these two verses together as one unified idea?

_____

_____

_____

Rob writes, "What a wonderful word is that little preposition—*through*."

What's the significance of the word "through" in this verse?

_____

_____

_____

_____

At what point does this phrase, "valley of the shadow of death" occur in Psalm 23? At the beginning? At the end? What significance is there in its position within the Psalm?

_____

_____

_____

Pastor Morgan also indicates the word shadow is also significant. Explain, in your own words, how this impacts the meaning of verse 4:

_____

_____

_____

Rob points out, what he calls a "dramatic change of the pronouns".

Read verses 1–3, circling the personal pronouns referring to God (i.e. he, you, your, his, etc.):

> The Lord is my shepherd; I shall not want.
> He makes me to lie down in green pastures; He leads me beside the still waters.
> He restores my soul;
> He leads me in the paths of righteousness for His name's sake.

Now read verses 4–6, circling the personal pronouns referring to God (i.e. he, you, your, his, etc.):

> Yea, though I walk through the valley of the shadow of death, I will fear no evil;
> For You are with me; Your rod and Your staff, they comfort me.
> You prepare a table before me in the presence of my enemies;
> You anoint my head with oil; my cup runs over.
> Surely goodness and mercy shall follow me all the days of my life.
> And I will dwell in the house of the Lord forever.

What about the pronouns changed, and why is this significant?

_____

_____

_____

_____

Pastor Morgan rephrases "Your rod and your staff, they comfort me" like this:

> *I am reassured by the shepherd's equipment. He isn't ill prepared. He has a rod to drive off predators and enemies. He knows how to club the foes that attack me. He also has a staff with the crooked or curved top, so He can snag and snatch me if I get too close to the edge of a precipice. He knows how to restrain my footsteps, how to protect me even from myself and my missteps.*

Are there other elements to the "shepherd's equipment" that are a comfort to you? Write your own rephrasing of "Your rod and your staff, they comfort me".

_____

_____

_____

HEAR THE SHEPHERD'S VOICE

As we noted above, the Wadi Kelt was likely the scene in David's mind as he penned verse 4. Rob notes this stretch of the route to Jerusalem from Jericho was called "the Way of Blood" due to the treachery of bandits and wild animals.

Read Matthew 20:17–19, 29. Why is it significant that Jesus travelled this route on the way to Jerusalem just before His crucifixion?

_____

_____

Rob writes, "The locomotive force of the wrath of a holy God hit Jesus Christ as He hung on Calvary's cross on Good Friday...The Good Shepherd laid down His life for his sheep and bore our death full force. As a result, we're hit only by the *shadow* of death."

Read John 11:25–26 and John 14:19 and explain how they coincide with Rob's remarks:

_____

_____

_____

_____

Read Acts 7:55–60. Notice that Stephen, facing death, in his dying moments reflects the phrase "I will fear no evil".

Name a few other Biblical characters or events mirror this sentiment?

_____

_____

_____

Read the following passages and note the impact they should have on your own outlook:

> *Deuteronomy 31:7–8*
> *Joshua 1:5, 9*
> *Hebrews 13:5–6*

_____

_____

_____

_____

FOLLOW THE SHEPHERD'S LEAD

We're certain to face valleys in this life, but we've learned a great deal about God's presence, His provision, and His protection, not to mention the temporal nature of difficulty.

How does this verse affect your outlook in your own "valley"?

_____

_____

_____

_____

Go back to the beginning of this lesson where you described the difficulty you're facing, and next to it, in big, bold letters, write the word: TEMPORARY.

Rob writes, "For Christians, problems are always temporary and blessings always eternal (as opposed to non-Christians, whose blessings are temporal and whose problems are eternal)." While this is comforting, it should also be troubling as we realize how much of the world still walks in darkness. Take a few moments to pray for the unsaved in the world, including those you know.

Concerning the phrase "I will fear no evil", Pastor Morgan writes "The reality of Psalm 23:4 removes the element of existential fear from the life of the Christian."

How can you deal with the fear you're experiencing?

_____

_____

_____

_____

REMEMBER THE SHEPHERD'S GOODNESS

Create a journal entry describing your "valley". What feelings and emotions are you experiencing? How does Psalm 23:4 change the equation? If you're not currently in a "valley", write out some insights you've gained through exploring this verse. Blank journal pages are provided for Lesson #6 beginning on page 85 in the back of this study guide.

Heavenly Father,
I thank you that you never leave or forsake me, even when I walk through dark valleys and difficult days. Thank you that, because of Jesus, my problems are temporary and my blessings are eternal. Comfort me with your presence, your provision, and your protection.
In Jesus' name, Amen

"If you're in a valley right now, look around. There beside you is the Good Shepherd. He's holding a rod in one hand, a staff in the other, and you're in His line of sight. You can talk to Him any time and always. You can pray, for the Good Shepherd gives His presence in life's valleys."
—Robert J. Morgan

The LORD is My SHEPHERD

STUDY GUIDE

The LORD *is My* SHEPHERD

LESSON 7

HIS PROVISION ON LIFE'S TABLELAND

You prepare a table for me in the presence of my enemies

Pastor Morgan opens chapter 8 with a story about Donald Britt, a veteran of World War II, who was once captured by German forces along with some of his fellow soldiers. After their capture, someone read the text of Psalm 23 aloud, which had a calming effect on all of them. As Christmas Eve approached, they sang Christmas Carols, hoping the guards would be moved by them. Their plan worked, and the guards gave them water served out of helmets. Morgan writes, "...the hearts of frightened boys were calmed by Psalm 23, read in the presence of their enemies, and...by God's grace their thirst was quenched when their helmets overflowed on Christmas Eve."

We may not all be in constant danger from an opposing army, but we all have enemies.

Who or what is the biggest enemy you face right now?

_____

What do you feel you need most as you face this enemy?

_____

_____

_____

_____

The unfortunate truth is, we have enemies of various kinds. But the good news we find in verse 5 is that this reality doesn't thwart the provision of our shepherd. Psalm 23:5 tells us:

You prepare a table for me in the presence of my enemies.

Let's look at this verse more closely.

Survey the Shepherd's Land

Read chapter 8 in The Lord is My Shepherd.

Read Psalm 23:5 several times.

According to Pastor Morgan, what's the significance of the word table in this verse?

_____

_____

How does he describe the geographic "progress" from verses 1–5?

_____

_____

What dangers does Morgan note that existed in these tablelands?

_____

_____

HEAR THE SHEPHERD'S VOICE

Pastor Rob notes that the key idea behind this verse is God's protection of His flock. He notes three kinds of enemies from whom we need protection.

To re-emphasize each in your mind, scan through chapter 8 and fill in the blanks:

1. *We Have* _____ *Enemies*
2. *We Have* _____ *Enemies*
3. *We Have* _____ *Enemies*

Read the following passages and remark as to how they affect your attitude towards personal enemies:

Matthew 5:33–48
Proverbs 19:11
Hebrews 12:15
Romans 12:18–19

_____

_____

_____

_____

Read the following verses. How do these passages affect your outlook on spiritual enemies?

> *Ephesians 6:12*
> *1 Corinthians 15:25*
> *John 10:27–29*

_____

_____

Read Isaiah 53:7 and John 10:15. What's the significance of Jesus' posture towards his enemies?

_____

_____

Does Jesus currently and will he always assume this posture towards His enemies? Read 1 Corinthians 15:25 and Revelation 11:5; 19:6 and explain why not:

_____

_____

FOLLOW THE SHEPHERD'S LEAD

In this world, we can't escape the reality of our enemies, but we can enjoy the Lord's provision despite them. We can allow the Good Shepherd to inform our outlook on national, personal, and spiritual enemies.

If the enemy you listed at the beginning of this lesson is personal, what steps can you take to love him or her?

_____

_____

If your enemy is hostile to the point where it goes beyond "as far as it depends on you" to live at peace (see Romans 12:18–19), describe how the Lord has prepared a table for you despite the enemy.

Detail the provision and blessings you enjoy:

_____

_____

_____

_____

What spiritual enemies do you face, and how has the Lord equipped you to deal with them?

_____

_____

_____

_____

REMEMBER THE SHEPHERD'S GOODNESS

Write a journal entry dealing your struggle against enemies. Describe the enemies you face, the difficulty they pose, and the emotions you experience. Then detail the Lord's provision and blessings in your life despite them. Blank journal pages are provided for Lesson #7 beginning on page 87 in the back of this study guide.

Heavenly Father,

Thank you that through Jesus Christ, I have ultimate victory over all my physical and spiritual enemies. Yet, Lord, it's difficult to live in a world where they're still present. I ask that you change the hearts of my personal enemies. If I can be a witness of your grace to them, I'm willing. But if it's beyond my ability, I ask you to soften their hearts and turn them to you before it's too late. I ask that you guard me against spiritual enemies who aim to deter my faith.

Deliver me from the evil one.

In Jesus' name, Amen

"Our Lord Jesus Christ gives us the provisions of safety and victory on life's tableland. Because of Him, we can live on the heights without fear. He spreads a table for us in the presence of our enemies."—Robert J. Morgan

The LORD is My SHEPHERD

LESSON 8

HIS POTION FOR LIFE'S HURTS

You anoint my head with oil; my cup runs over

Pastor Morgan begins chapter 9 with a story about his sheep rancher friend named Duane. Duane purchased an ewe who wouldn't have anything to do with him. That is, until she injured her foot and fell ill. Through his tending to her wounds and the healing process, she's learned to trust him completely.

Likewise, as Rob points out, "It's often during life's hurts that we come to understand the heart of the Shepherd, as we learn to accept His care and to trust His heart. As He tends us and mends us, we fall in love with Him and receive the comfort He gives."

What hurts are you currently experiencing in your life?

_____

_____

_____

_____

Is it difficult for you to entrust these hurts to the care of Jesus as your shepherd? Why or why not?

_____

_____

_____

As Rob says, "Troubles in life have a way of driving us to the Lord's tender mercies, and we bond with Him through the verses and vigor He bestows". Psalm 23:5 ends with this phrase:

You anoint my head with oil; my cup runs over.

Let's discover how this plays out in Scripture and in our lives.

SURVEY THE SHEPHERD'S LAND

Read chapter 9 in The *Lord is My Shepherd*.

Read Psalm 23:5 several times, focusing on the last two statements.

What ministry of the Good Shepherd is in view when the Psalm says "You anoint my head with oil; my cup runs over"?

_____

_____

What does anointing with oil have to do with tending literal sheep? What's the implication in our lives as believers?

_____

_____

What's the significance of an overflowing cup to a sheep? How does this affect your understanding of what our Good Shepherd offers us?

_____

_____

_____

Pastor Morgan rephrases Psalm 23:5 in this way:

> *God's blessings have been poured out into my life so greatly that they overflow. I can't contain all of them. I can't absorb all the mercy and goodness that He has given me. I may not understand all it has cost My shepherd to provide such blessings, but I live in constant thanksgiving that my trough overflows. Goodness and mercy are certainly following me all the days of my life.*

Rephrase verse 5 in your own words:

_____

_____

_____

HEAR THE SHEPHERD'S VOICE

Pastor Rob writes, "Psalm 23:5 speaks of the tending ministries of the Good Shepherd when it says, "You anoint my head with oil; my cup runs over".

Read Isaiah 40:11 and Ezekiel 34:11–16.

What does this teach us about what shepherds do for their sheep and what the Lord does for us?

_____

_____

Morgan notes, "In the Bible, the words *Christ* and *Messiah* mean the 'Anointed One'".

What "oil" was Jesus anointed with? Read the following passages to inform your answer:

> Isaiah 61:1–3
> Psalm 45:7
> Isaiah 11:2
> Matthew 3:16
> John 3:34

_____

_____

_____

How do we, as Christ's sheep, experience the anointing of His Spirit? Read the following passages to inform your answer:

> John 14:16–17
> Galatians 5:16–18
> Romans 14:17

_____

_____

_____

_____

Read John 4:14, John 7:37–38, and Romans 15:13. Describe, in your own words, the "overflowing cup" offered to us by Christ:

_____

_____

_____

FOLLOW THE SHEPHERD'S LEAD

When we feel hurt, we often also feel alone. Psalm 23:5 reminds us that our shepherd is ready and willing to *tend* to us as His flock. Let's look at some practical implications on our lives.

Write a brief prayer, committing your hurts into the hands of Jesus, the Good Shepherd:

_____

_____

_____

_____

How does understanding the anointing and empowering role of the Holy Spirit affect your approach to life's hurts?

_____

_____

Rob writes, "The Christian life is the overflowing life, and there's an important implication to that. As laborers in the Kingdom, our *work* for the Lord is simply the overflow of our *walk* with Him."

Describe how you could improve your commitment to walking with the Lord:

_____

_____

_____

_____

REMEMBER THE SHEPHERD'S GOODNESS

Journal today about the hurts you face in your life right now. Be honest and open in describing your experience. Detail how your understanding of the tending ministry of Jesus offers answers to dealing with these hurts. Blank journal pages are provided for Lesson #8 beginning on page 89 in the back of this study guide.

> *Heavenly Father,*
> *You truly are the Good Shepherd, for you're aware of every hurt in my life and you tend to them. Forgive me where I've attempted to mend my wounds through my own devices. I want to grow closer to you through life's painful experiences. I need your healing. Please fill my cup overflowing with the Holy Spirit, that you might be glorified in me today and every day.*
> *In Jesus' name, Amen*

"Because Jesus drained His cup, ours can overflow. All our blessings in this life and the next—all were purchased for us by the Good Shepherd when He laid down His life for His sheep."—Robert J. Morgan

The LORD is My SHEPHERD

LESSON 9

HIS PROMISES FOR LIFE'S JOURNEYS

Surely goodness and mercy shall follow me all the days of my life

I grew up around dogs. My favorite dog was probably our Cocker Spaniel named "Shadow". It was an appropriate name not only because he had dark black fur, but also because he was always right next to you. You could go anywhere and Shadow would follow you, not leaving your side.

Rob makes a case that in Psalm 23, David's thoughts go "to the dogs" so to speak. That in his mind, David envisions the pursuing nature of sheep herding dogs who surround the shepherd's people with goodness and mercy.

What evidence of goodness and mercy are you seeing in your life currently?

_____

_____

_____

_____

The good news is that our Good Shepherd has no intention of calling off the dogs. Psalm 23:6 begins with this phrase:

Surely goodness and mercy shall follow me all the days of my life.

We've made our way through trenches and valleys, past tablelands where enemies may surround us. Now we're finding that it's not enemies who are most persistent, it's the shepherd's goodness and mercy! Let's explore these blessings together.

SURVEY THE SHEPHERD'S LAND

Read chapter 10 in *The Lord is My Shepherd*.

Read Psalm 23:6 several times, focusing on the first statement.

Pastor Morgan bases his suggestion, that David had sheepdogs in mind in verse 6, based on the verb "follow". Read Rob's explanation and write down the other translations he suggests for "follow":

_____

_____

_____

_____

How does it affect your thinking to imagine goodness and mercy as sheepdogs, hunting and pursuing you, surrounding you no matter where you turn?

_____

_____

_____

What's impact does the word surely have on this text and on your life?

_____

_____

How does Pastor Morgan define goodness and mercy? How would you explain these concepts to someone else?

_____

_____

_____

_____

_____

How does the phrase "all the days of my life" impact the meaning and application of this verse?

_____

_____

_____

HEAR THE SHEPHERD'S VOICE

The word "surely", Rob explains, "has the basic meaning of 'no doubt; this is absolutely true; this can never be doubted; it can never fail." He adds, "The Bible is full of terminology that conveys the confidence we should have in our Lord and His Word."

Read the following passages and note their implication in your life:

> *Romans 8:38–39*
> *Job 19:25*
> *2 Corinthians 2:3, 5:6–8*
> *1 John 5:13–14*
> *Romans 4:16–22*

_____

_____

_____

_____

In describing goodness and mercy, Pastor Morgan says, "Goodness represents all He bestows on us that we *don't* deserve. Mercy represents all He withholds that we *do* deserve".

How do goodness and mercy find their ultimate fulfillment in Jesus Christ, the Good Shepherd who laid down His life for His sheep?

_____

_____

_____

Scripture is full of references to the goodness and mercy poured out on us by God. Morgan notes "This theme in the Bible has literally changed my personality".

Read the following passages, writing down any new perspective you gain:

> *John 10:10–11*
> *Psalm 21:3, 34:10, 84:11, 100:3*
> *Matthew 7:11*
> *James 1:17*
> *John 1:16*
> *Ephesians 1:3*

_____

_____

_____

Rob points out this verse as one of the Bible's great "all"s.

Explain how verses like this one and Romans 8:28 can possibly be so extensive in their application:

_____

_____

_____

FOLLOW THE SHEPHERD'S LEAD

As we near the end of our journey through the various seasons and pathways of life in Psalm 23, we're introduced to a vivid truth, that we're being hunted, pursued, chased—not by an enemy, but by goodness and mercy. We're told this will remain true throughout our lives!

How does this imagery impact your approach to life's difficulties?

_____

_____

_____

If you tend to worry about your future, describe how the words "all the days of my life" can counteract your worries:

_____

_____

_____

REMEMBER THE SHEPHERD'S GOODNESS

Write a journal entry describing the goodness and mercy that follow you and will continue to do so throughout life. Blank journal pages are provided for Lesson #9 beginning on page 91 in the back of this study guide.

> *Heavenly Father,*
> *Thank you for pursuing me with your goodness and mercy. Because of Jesus, I've not received the wrath I deserve and I've received blessings I do not deserve in and of myself. Thank you for the confidence I have that you will continue to pursue me with goodness and mercy for all my days. Help me live a life worthy of such blessings.*
> *In Jesus' name, Amen*

"The mercy of the Lord is everlasting to everlasting on those who fear Him, and His righteousness to children's children" (Psalm 103:17, NKJV).

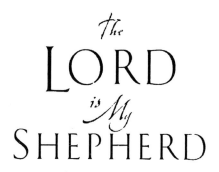

The LORD *is My* SHEPHERD

LESSON 10

HIS PALACES AT LIFE'S END

And I will dwell in the house of the Lord forever

When I was a kid, my family once went on a trip to a little place in Chattanooga Tennessee called "Rock City". The problem was, with my four sisters and me in the car, every road trip was sure to be a challenge! On the way to Rock City, there are dozens of billboards for the attraction, including advertisements painted on birdhouses and barns. My parents encouraged us to play a game, competing for "points" by being the first to yell "See Rock City!" when we saw one of the signs. I got so caught up in the game I didn't realize that I was only enjoying the signs and forgetting about the actual destination!

We've come to the last stop at the end of our trek—our destination. We've seen how the Lord is our shepherd, leading us and providing for us through every season of life. But now it's time to really take time to explore our ultimate and eternal destination: the house of the Lord.

When you think of following the Good Shepherd into your eternal home, do you anticipate it with joy? Do you fear you'll be losing something you currently have—possessions, experiences, or relationships? Describe your honest reaction:

_____

_____

_____

Our journey with the Good Shepherd does have a final destination, and it's an eternal one. Psalm 23:6 ends with this:

And I will dwell in the house of the Lord forever.

Pastor Morgan reminds us that in Psalm 23 we see:

> *Beside Me: My Shepherd*
> *Beneath Me: Green Pastures*
> *Near Me: Still Waters*
> *Ahead of Me: Righteous Paths*
> *Within Me: Restored Spirits*
> *Against Me: My Enemies*
> *For Me: His Rod and Staff*
> *Around Me: A Tableland*
> *Upon Me: Anointing Oil*
> *Above Me: Overflowing Blessings*
> *Behind Me: Goodness and Mercy*
> *Before Me: My Father's House*

Let's look at this final step together:

Survey the Shepherd's Land

Read chapter 11 in The Lord is My Shepherd.

Read Psalm 23:6 several times, focusing on the last statement.

What literal place is King David thinking of in this last statement in Psalm 23:6 when he refers to "the house of the Lord"?

_____

As we "survey the land", let's look at other biblical passages concerning this phrase "the house of the Lord". Read the following passages:

Psalm 27:2
Psalm 92:12–13
Psalm 122:1
Exodus 23:19
1 Samuel 1:7, 24
1 Kings 7:41, 8:11

In these passages, what is the house of the Lord?

_____

_____

Is the "house of the Lord" a description of a physical building, or does it refer more to the dwelling place of God? Read Acts 17:24 to inform your answer:

_____

How does Revelation 21:3 describe the tabernacle (dwelling place) of the Lord?

_____

_____

How does Jesus describe this place in John 14:1–3 and Luke 23:43?

_____

_____

Read Revelation 21 and 22 and describe, in your own words, what scenery stands out in your mind:

_____

_____

Hear the Shepherd's Voice

Rob points out that Psalm 23 begins with "The Lord" and ends with "forever". Yet it's sometimes difficult for us to understand how the Lord expects His sheep to live with an eternal perspective. Hebrews 11 offers us some guidance here.

Read Hebrews 11:1–16. Rephrase verse 16 in your own words:

_____

_____

_____

Now put Hebrews 11:16 in personal language as it pertains to your own life as the shepherd calls you to a life of faith:

_____

_____

_____

Follow the Shepherd's Lead

Pause and take a moment to reflect on the *house of the Lord* as your ultimate, eternal destination. Let your meditation flow into prayer and praise.

How does it affect you in the current season of life you're in, to reflect on these truths?

_____

_____

What steps can you take to live with the wholehearted expectation and anticipation of a heavenly destination?

_____

_____

_____

_____

REMEMBER THE SHEPHERD'S GOODNESS

As you ponder your ultimate destination, record a journal entry detailing your thoughts, emotions, and commitments based on the truth: "And I will dwell in the house of the Lord forever". Blank journal pages are provided for Lesson #10 beginning on page 93 in the back of this study guide.

> *Heavenly Father,*
> *Through life's twists and turns, you lead me as my faithful, Good Shepherd. I cannot describe the wonder and awe that overwhelms me when I embrace the place you've prepared, eternally dwelling in your presence. But I must admit sometimes it's hard to truly place my focus and my hope in that future because of where I am now. Help me in my unbelief, and please continue to lead me on that path until I reach the house of the Lord.*
> *In Jesus' name, Amen*

"Never forget that the last word of Psalm 23 is the first word of eternity."
—Robert J. Morgan

The
LORD
is My
SHEPHERD
STUDY GUIDE

Lesson 1

Lesson 2

Lesson 3

Lesson 4

Lesson 5

Lesson 6

Lesson 7

Lesson 8

Lesson 9

Lesson 10

CPSIA information can be obtained at www.ICGtesting.com
Printed in the USA
LVOW101802210413

329929LV00002B/2/P